P9-DMI-675

This delightful book is the latest in the series of Ladybird books that have been specially planned to help grown-ups with the world about them.

As in the other books in this series, the large, clear script, the careful choice of words, the frequent repetition and the thoughtful matching of text with pictures all enable grown-ups to think they have taught themselves to cope. The subject of the book will greatly appeal to grown-ups.

Series 999

THE LADYBIRD
BOOKS FOR GROWN-UPS SERIES

THE
HANGOVER

by

J. A. HAZELEY, N.S.F.W. and J. P. MORRIS, O.M.G.

(Authors of 'Bedroom Secrets of the Boardroom Batman')

Publishers: Ladybird Books Ltd, Loughborough
Printed in England. If wet, Italy.

Sometimes, when we drink too much, we get a hangover.

There is no cure for the hangover, but it can be treated with a cup of strong coffee and a couple of fried breakfasts.

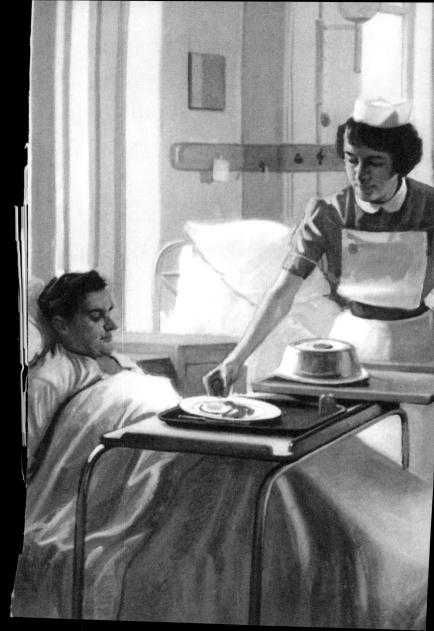

A good hangover should be a total mystery to you.

How did this happen? Why do you feel so ill?

Pretend to yourself that you drank less than you did. Insist you stuck to beer, forgetting the champagne at the start of the evening and the round of jalapeño tequilas you did for a bet in that club next to the dual carriageway at 2 a.m.

Some hangover symptoms are caused by impurities which enter the body along with the alcohol.

These impurities can include methanol, acetone, acetaldehyde, esters, tannins, grab bags of Wotsits, railway-grade pasties and KFC Zinger Tower Burgers.

What a confusing world it can seem with a hangover.

Sit as still as you can. Do not attempt to make any decisions.

Look out of the window. Can you recognise simple shapes or colours? Is there a moon or a sun in the sky? What sort of a name might you have? Where might there be bacon?

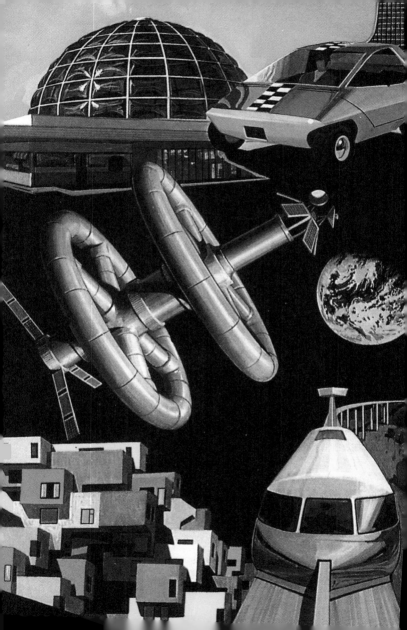

Consuming alcohol lowers the body's reserves of vital elements such as iron, potassium, water and bacon.

Every unit of alcohol kills the equivalent of two inches of bacon, which must be replaced the next morning.

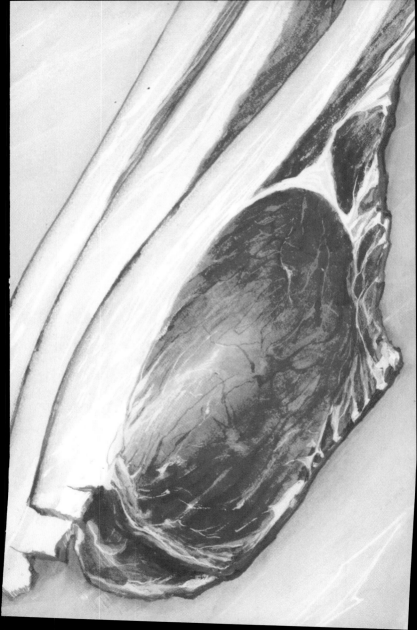

Prepare a hangover first-aid kit of a banana and a pint of water to put by your bedside before going out for an evening's drinking.

When you wake, fully dressed, the next morning, you can look at the untouched glass and the uneaten banana and wonder who left them there, and why.

Peggy is trying "the hair of the dog" to get rid of her hangover.

She was drinking gin last night, so a sip from the gin bottle will help put her body back in balance.

Peggy does not know where the recorder came from. She does remember stealing a busker's hat for her cab fare home. Maybe that explains it.

Len's mouth feels like he fell asleep tongue-first on an antique bear pelt. His heart is galloping, his hair aches, and he worries that there is sweat building up underneath his fingernails.

Len has come outside for some fresh air, but now remembers he is scared of fresh air today.

Maybe the policeman can help.

"Can I get you a drink, Len?" asks the policeman.

Michael is bored. Mummy has not moved since she put the DVD on.

The menu screen has been going round and round for two hours. Mummy forgot to press play.

Michael should not have woken poor Mummy up so early.

Friday night work drinks went on longer than expected. Ron has a head like a smelting works full of howler monkeys on ephedrine.

Ron is glad Saturday mornings require little more than the vocabulary, reasoning and motor skills of a seven-year-old. Ron is happy on the floor.

Later, he will try to buy a bulb of garlic at a self-service checkout and will burst into tears.

The morning after the party, Emeric is woken by a stray cat licking his face. He has slept under a hedge and cannot remember a thing.

Emeric uses street signs and clues from his clothing to piece together where he lives and what he does for a living.

Emeric hopes it was a fancy-dress party. If these are his work clothes, no wonder he needed to drink.

The morning after a wedding, everybody feels a little the worse for wear.

It can seem like there are no grown-ups left in charge. What will happen? Who will help us? Is this the end? What if the Earth crashes into the Sun?

Do not panic. Soon the hangover will be over, and you can all celebrate with a nice drink.

Going to work with a hangover might seem impossible, but it is important that you do not lose your job. Even if that was the reason you got drunk.

Try to turn up at the usual time, say hello to everyone, then have a little nap somewhere quiet such as the roof.

What's the worst that could happen?

Hector knows the best way to avoid a hangover is to remember how bad he felt the last time he drank too much wine.

Sadly, after the first glass of wine, Hector remembers feeling quite good. And the next glass makes him feel even better.

"I feel invincible," roars Hector.

Try not to drive or operate heavy machinery with a hangover.

Last night, Bernie and his crew celebrated winning the works' canteen quiz.

Now they are going to have to build this part of the hospital again.

Susan woke up next to a full glass of wine. She left it by the bedside in case she became thirsty in the night.

Now Susan does not know whose flat it was or where the nearest station might be.

At least she is dressed properly in case there is another party on the walk home.

This cat is judging you.

Get off the floor.

And put some underwear on.

If you are drinking something unfamiliar, be prepared for it to affect you in unexpected ways.

The distillation acts of the seventeenth century introduced gin to many British towns for the first time.

This is Canterbury.

Tony took £150 out from the cash machine after work. He woke up drenched in sweat with loose change all over his bed.

Tony hopes the many, many coins will be enough to go and buy an important breakfast.

Tony has 72p.

Most shops offer refunds for purchases you discover you made while drunk, as long as you keep the packaging and receipt.

For younger people, a hangover's symptoms are mainly physical.

The body is listless, the head is sore, they crave food for no reason, and spend a long time in the toilet.

For older people, this is perfectly normal. So, for them, a hangover is more spiritual.

The morning after consuming alcohol, you may find you are more sensitive to noise.

Some people can actually "see" sounds. It is almost as if drinking gives you superpowers!

While the effect wears off, remember, you do not have to get out of the way of birdsong, or duck when someone calls your name.

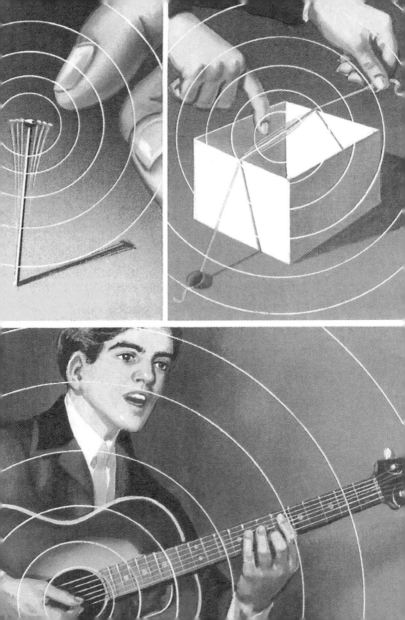

There are lots of ways to avoid a hangover.

Try vomiting regularly into a bag. Put a brick on the bag and keep vomiting until the bag is full enough to tip it over.

Or set yourself limits. Try drinking only what you can get into your body without touching the container. This is also a good way of turning drinking from a chore into a game.

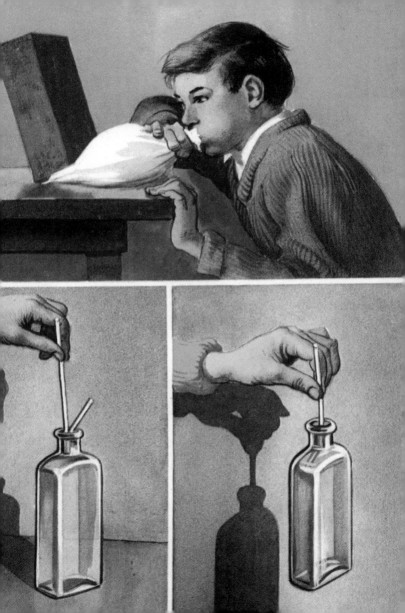

Winston Churchill was prime minister of Britain from 1940 to 1945, and again from 1951 to 1955. He was First Lord of the Admiralty in the Great War, won the Nobel Prize in Literature, and led the Allies to defeat Nazi Germany in the Second World War.

He had a persistent, nagging hangover from 1892 to 1965, when he died.

He never surrendered.

The authors would like to thank the illustrators whose work they have so mercilessly ribbed, and whose glorious craftsmanship was the set-dressing of their childhoods. The inspiration they sparked has never faded.

MICHAEL JOSEPH

UK | USA | Canada | Ireland | Australia
India | New Zealand | South Africa

Michael Joseph is part of the Penguin Random House group of companies whose addresses can be found at global.penguinrandomhouse.com

First published 2015
001

Copyright © Jason Hazeley and Joel Morris, 2015
All images copyright © Ladybird Books Ltd, 2015

The moral right of the authors has been asserted

Printed in Italy by L.E.G.O. S.p.A

A CIP catalogue record for this book is available from the British Library

ISBN: 978–0–718–18351–6

www.greenpenguin.co.uk

MIX
Paper from
responsible sources
FSC® C018179

Penguin Random House is committed to a sustainable future for our business, our readers and our planet. This book is made from Forest Stewardship Council® certified paper.